Mouthguards & Sport Safety

A Unique, One-Stop, Practical, No-Nonsense Resource for Everyone Who Recommends or Should Wear a Mouthguard

ISBN 978-0-9578929-0-3 (PDF Version)
ISBN 978-0-9578929-1-0 (Print Version)

1. Medical Science – Dentistry 2. Sports & Games 3. Education 4. Sports Safety

A catalogue record for this publication is
available from the National Library of Australia

Good Innovations publications may be purchased for educational,
business or sales promotional use.
For more information please email: info@mouthguardsafety.com

Produced by

◌ Good Innovations

www.goodinnovations.com

1

About the Author

Julian Hodges BA DMS has no formal dental qualifications yet he is one of the world's foremost mouthguard experts.

20 Years ago he realised that most mouthguards did not provide enough protection and that there would be fewer dental injuries in sport – fewer broken teeth, facial scarring and fractured jaws – if there were better mouthguards. Since then he has studied, reviewed, analysed, tested, developed skills and learned from the foremost experts.

Now, in what you could say is a true test, specialists from around the world seek his advice. He has spoken, published, consulted and coached to acclaim in Australasia, the Pacific, Europe, Asia, and the United States. He has advised sports people, sporting associations, parents, trainers, coaches, dentists as well as universities, colleges, hospitals, the military and dental laboratories including the worlds largest.

Julian Hodges teaches and instructs dentists and dental technicians how to make super comfortable, highly protective mouthguards. He has been described as, *"Unique in his field"* and, *"A Coach that achieves outstanding results."*

His research proved to the Australian Health Authorities, and to others, that there is a need for standards for mouthguards. Consequently Julian Hodges is a Founder Member of the Standards Australia Technical Committee for Sports Mouthguards and the specialist advisor for the Australian Dental Industries Association.

In Summary: Julian Hodges knows mouthguards and how to deliver protection to sports people irrespective of their age, sport or level of competition. He presents, what can be a complex subject, in a simple, balanced, practical way that can be immediately and easily understood and implemented.

Disclaimer

Mouthguard protection is always a matter for specialist professional dental and medical advice for each individual.

This manual recommends from the outset individual specialist dental and medical advice for all persons considering mouthguard usage.

None of the content within this manual is intended as any substitution for specialist dental and medical advice and each person should rely upon their own private dental and medical consultants in that regard.

The content and commentary within this manual is by way of general guideline only. This manual is directed towards the strongest recommendation for properly chosen and fitted mouthguards to be worn by persons involved with certain physical activities. **Each individual should consult his or her specialist dental or medical advisor for special advice on appropriate mouthguard applications for each individual.** The information herein is not held out as to accuracy, specifically or generally.

Contents

What You Need to Know to Minimise or Eliminate Dental Injuries in Sport

The reason you need this handbook

The sole intention of this Handbook is to reduce dental injuries in sport. 'Mouthguards and Mouthguard Safety' will give you information only a few people know. It is written in easy to understand, non-technical terms and will to help you assess and select the right mouthguards.

In many ways you will know as much as the professionals and, as a bonus, you or those that you lead, will play better and enjoy sport more.

It is important you realistically consider the degree of impact or collision that may occur when competing or training.

Do you know the risk you are taking by not wearing a mouthguard?

Do these facts apply to you and, are you putting yourself in danger of permanent damage or disfigurement?

- There is a **95% chance of permanent disfigurement to your most visible upper front teeth** when you have an injury to your teeth.

- **31%** of sporting injuries will result in damage to your **teeth, face and head**.

- In the USA over 200,000 oral injuries are prevented annually by sports mouthguards which is tremendous. But unfortunately, mouthguard usage is so low that **25 times** more teeth are lost in sporting activity. That is more than **5,000,000** teeth per year!

- In American Football, where mouthguards are compulsory, only **0.07%** of all injuries involve teeth and the mouth but, in Basketball, where they are not compulsory, and mouthguards are not worn, the injury rate is **34%**.

So, the problem is serious and you may be in considerably more danger than you realise.

82% of mouthguards are "an accident waiting to happen"

I estimate that 82% of mouthguards can be considered *An Accident Waiting to Happen!* And the probability is – yours is one of them.

I know that you are looking for the best protection and value for money. But, are you *really* getting the best protection? Saving Money? Maybe not! How do you know?

It is currently estimated that if you lose a tooth, it will cost you $30,000 and possibly more in treatment expenses over your life. When this happens, in addition to the pain and disfigurement, what is the real cost of the mouthguard that you bought so cheaply?

Fortunately you can have a mouthguard that is made by a technique called *'Custom Laminating'*. It may give you up to **9 times more protection** than some Over the Counter 'Boil & Bite' mouthguards plus:

- The ability to breathe and speak with ease

- More choice

- More comfort

- A greater feeling of security

What is surprising is that this type of mouthguard has been available since 1982 but for many years few knew about them!

That is about to change. In this Handbook you will discover much more than you ever imagined about gaining oral protection, reducing dental injuries and playing with more confidence.

Concussion and mouthguards

Concussion can occur when your brain is forced against and hits your skull from the impact of a sudden blow or collision.

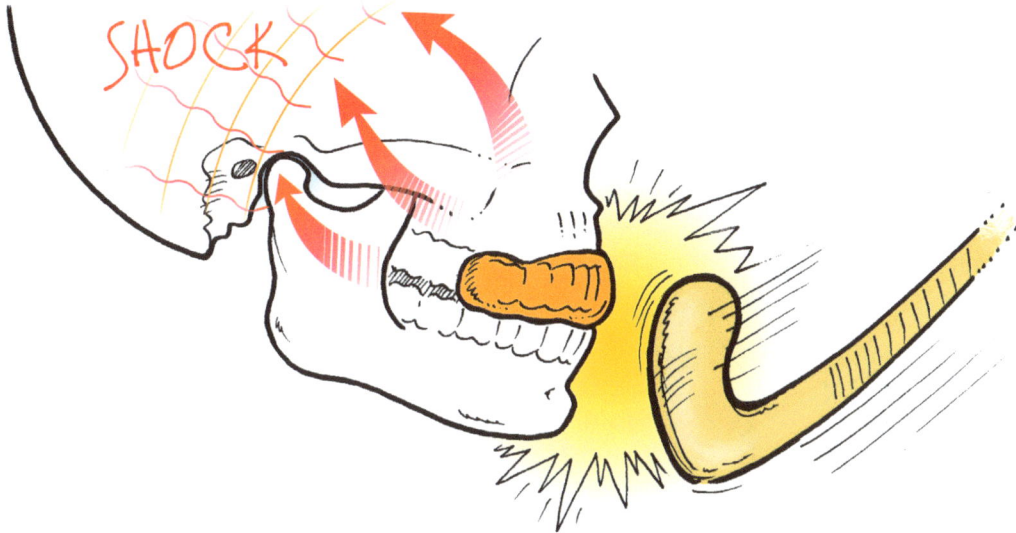

Depending on its severity, concussion may cause short and long term problems. You may experience confusion, loss of memory, loss of consciousness, severe headaches, sudden weakness, double vision and ringing in the ears.

There is increasing evidence, highlighted by the latest American research, that there may be a cumulative effect with repeated concussions. Additionally, once concussed, there may be a 4-fold increase in the risk of being concussed a second time.

Greater focus is being placed on correct recovery protocols. When this occurs, Dr Paul McCrory, a neurologist and Editor of the Journal of Sports Medicine considers there is no support for the statement that concussion (as seen in **sports**) is cumulative.

But, there is need for care! There are publications that state, mouthguards may reduce concussion and many mouthguard make the same claim. However, it is becoming apparent that they may not be correct. An increasing number of specialists consider the protective benefits of mouthguards against concussion are unsubstantiated. Again, according to Dr McCrory:

- The international expert consensus (see Vienna 2001 and Prague 2005 Consensus Statements) supports the statement that mouthguard do not prevent concussion

- Published randomised controlled trials in Australian Football and separately in Rugby Union have shown no scientific benefit from mouthguards in preventing concussion.

Irrespective of the extent of the claimed concussion reducing effect of mouthguards, *if it is suspected that a person may have been concussed, even slightly, seek immediate expert medical advice!*

Reducing tempormandibular (jaw joint) injuries

Depending upon the degree and direction of the impact from a blow, your lower jaw may be forced up and could damage the jaw joint (temporomandibular joint or TMJ).

A mouthguard creates a gap. This gap must be maintained even with light impact. In this way, the possibility of injury can be reduced.

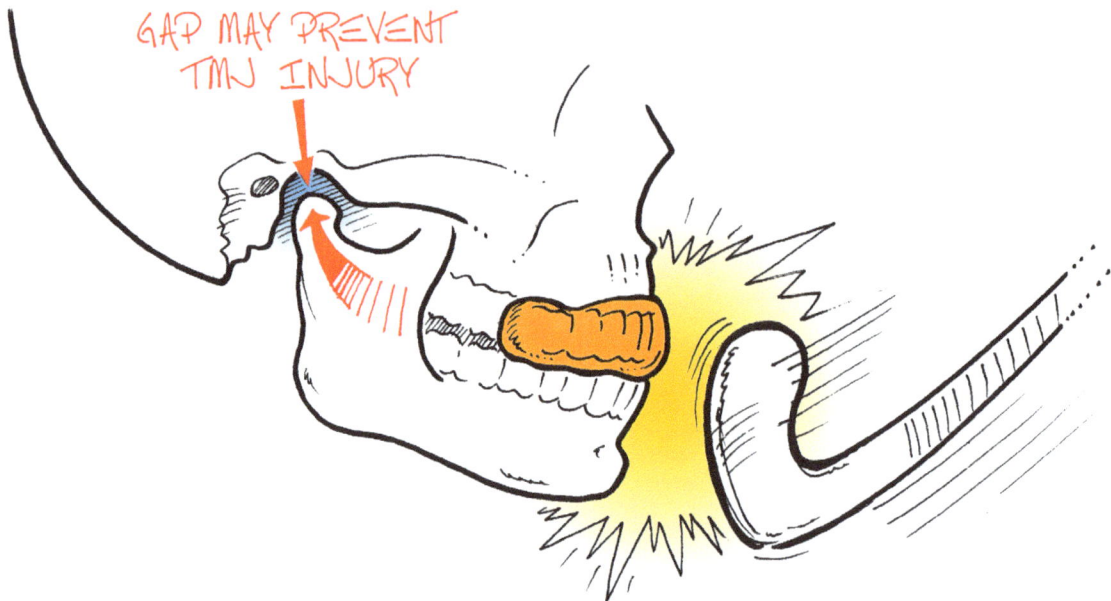

A poor mouthguard may not create a sufficient gap!!

How a mouthguard may help to reduce jaw injury

To understand how a mouthguard reduces jaw injury, you need to know how your mouthguard should function:

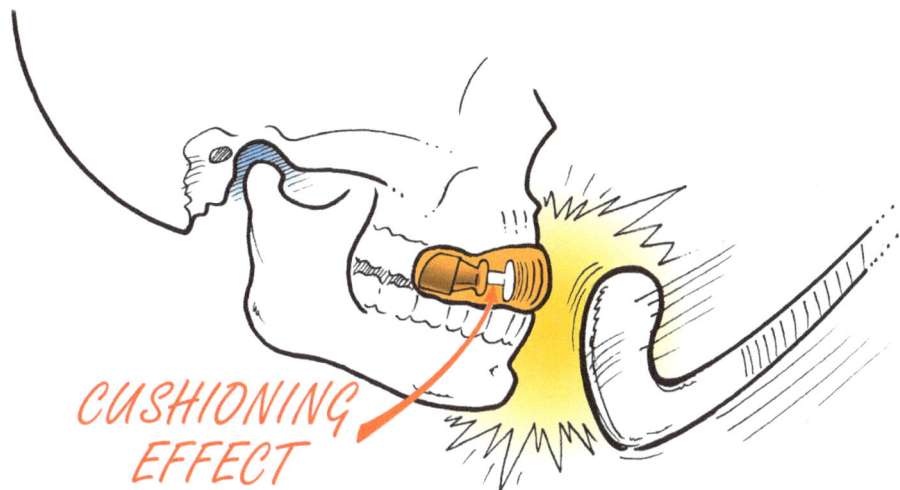

CUSHIONING EFFECT

- A properly fitted mouthguard should provide some cushioning effect from impact. Some of the force will be absorbed by the mouthguard material at the point of impact. **Remember it is not possible to totally absorb the force of a blow at the point of impact!**

  It is then that a mouthguard may provide some **'cushioning effect'** or a 'buffer'. It does this when it cushions impact over the whole mouthguard and distributes impact throughout your mouth, especially to your posterior (molar) teeth. These teeth have multiple roots. They act as anchors and provide the foundation for the cushioning effect.

  A poor mouthguard or one not fitted or worn correctly has a low cushioning effect!!

  Tests have proved that some mouthguards can provide **up to five times more total cushioning** than others.

- Your mouthguard needs to keep its shape and not be easily distorted with a blow. This is particularly important if you play heavy collision sports or sports with hard objects such as hockey sticks or racquets.

  A poor or poorly fitted or worn mouthguard has a low resistance to distortion!!

The most protective can provide up to **nine times more resistance** to distortion.

Why is fit so important?

"Schoolboy Swallows Mouthguard" – that was the headline in an Australian newspaper. Why did that mouthguard get stuck in the boy's throat? Because it became dislodged. The fit was not good enough! **It did not have enough retention.**

The fit of your mouthguard is vitally important for a number of reasons. A major reason is to avoid your mouthguard being suddenly dislodged by a blow. Another is to maximise the cushioning effect.

The amount of retention can vary dramatically! Back in 1997 university tests showed that, for one wearer, as little *as 3 grams (0.15 ounces)* was all that was needed to remove his mouthguard!

The tests conclusively proved that Custom Laminated Mouthguards have the **highest retention rates of all mouthguards**. And –

With the exception of a few high vacuum machines, mouthguards formed under pressure fit more accurately than mouthguards formed with vacuum.

If your mouthguard has the micron accuracy it should have, you will discover it will:

- Be much more comfortable

- Allow you to speak easily

- Allow you to breathe easily

- Give you more protection

Remember, the shape of your teeth and mouth is unique. No one is the same as you. So, don't be like that Australian Schoolboy – **Wear a mouthguard that is fitted and is unique for you!**

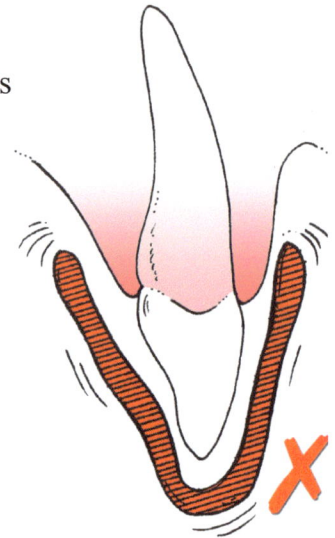

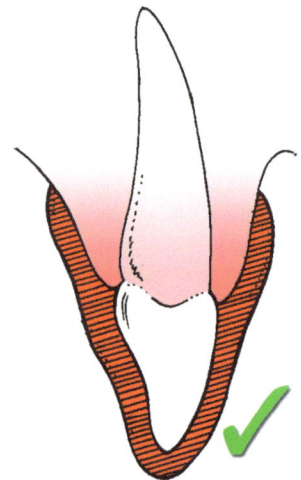

6 Important benefits of a mouthguard

Now you have a better knowledge of mouthguards, it is easier to understand that there are **6 important benefits you should ensure you have from your mouthguard.** It should:

- Help to reduce the possibility of being concussed and suffering brain damage.

- Provide you with more comfort and make it easier for you to breathe and speak.

- Enable you to compete more competitively and perform more confidently.

- Reduce the possibility of your teeth being fractured or lost.

- Reduce the possibility of your jaw being dislocated or fractured.

- Reduce the risk of cuts and bruising to your mouth and disfigurement to your face.

How much protection are you *Really* getting?

Do you know how much protection you are getting from your mouthguard? Probably not. And did the person or shop that supplied your mouthguard, know how protective it would be for you? Again, probably not.

Although every mouthguard is different, you need to know in comparative terms, how much protection you are getting and if your mouthguard is suitable for your sport and level of competition.

As you now know, tests in Germany showed that there can be up to 939% difference. But, before we look at the results we need to understand …

What are the different types of mouthguards?

Mouthguards are sometimes classified as Type I, II, III etc. But, to me there are 2 types:

- The type where the mouthguard <u>is formed in your mouth</u>.

- The type that is not. These are <u>made on a model of your mouth</u>.

There are many makers of the type that you buy Over The Counter (often called 'Boil & Bite') and are formed in your mouth. Claims may be made about their protection and comfort but for me 'Boil & Bite' mouthguards have:

2 Advantages

- They are relatively inexpensive

- They are convenient to buy

2 Major Disadvantages

- Protection is variable and <u>always inferior</u> to a good custom made mouthguard.

- It is almost <u>impossible,</u> if not impossible, to get a good fit and therefore sufficient retention. University tests have proved –
  Even a dental specialist cannot be sure to improve the retention in your mouth of a 'Boil & Bite' mouthguard!

This forces me to ask you, **'Why do you buy a mouthguard?'**

- If it is for convenience alone, then buy a 'Boil & Bite'.

- If it is for better protection, buy a well made Custom Laminated Mouthguard.

Now we have to ask the question –

Do ALL custom made mouthguards provide the protection you need?

Specialists universally recommend mouthguards that are custom made. But, do all custom made mouthguards provide the protection you need?

The answer is – *Some Do and, Some Don't!!*

Custom made mouthguards are made by specialists on a model of your mouth so you would expect them to be good. The best!

- A single piece of material can be used. It is heated and formed by vacuum or pressure. But, there is a problem that is **impossible to overcome!**

  There is, what is technically known as, the Thermoforming Effect. The result of this effect is that by using a single piece of material your mouthguard will always be thinner on the edges of your front teeth (it's called the incisal edge). But,

That is where you want maximum protection and not less!!

- The way to reduce the problem is to **custom laminate by individually forming and bonding two or more layers**. It's similar to laminating a car windscreen and has the same effect. MORE PROTECTION!! Considerably more protection than the single layer version.

- In addition, when multi-layers are formed and bonded, the Thermoforming Effect is overcome. MORE PROTECTION is provided just where single layer mouthguards are weakest! At your front teeth.

Thinning

Increased Protection

These are the major reasons why Custom Laminated Mouthguards are more protective than single layer mouthguards.
The proof is undeniable!

Tests have shown that with Custom Laminating but using the same amount of material, you can immediately have **22.5% more impact absorption and 43.6% more total cushioning**.

Unfortunately for those who don't know, there can be a catch. Some mouthguards are made from materials that are laminated **before** they are formed. The claim is that these are

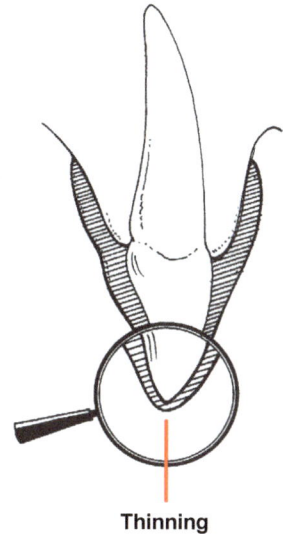

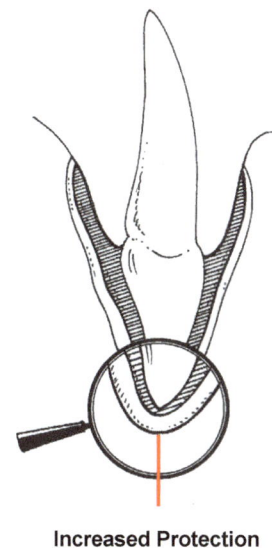

'laminated mouthguards'. They may be made from factory laminated materials, but they are not Custom Laminated.

Fortunately, you won't be fooled! Because you now know that:

It is only by individually forming and bonding each layer that protection is increased.

What are the most protective mouthguards ever tested?

One of the advantages of Custom Laminated Mouthguards is that we can use different types and thickness of materials. This makes it possible for a mouthguard to be designed and made that will suit you, your sport, the competition and the level of collision or impact.

The mouthguard you are wearing may be very good. But how good? You don't know, and nor does anyone else, unless the protection of that design and construction has been TESTED and compared to the protection from other mouthguards.

The mouthguards that we are going to assess have not only been INDEPENDENTLY TESTED but also TESTED MORE EXTENSIVELY than others. **They are proven to be more protective!**

The tests were conducted in Germany at the University of Tubingen with specially designed test equipment that amplified the effect of a blow to the teeth. In this way it was possible to measure how much power is distributed throughout the mouth by different mouthguards.

What you need to remember is this: *the more power (impact from a blow) that is distributed to your first molar, the less remains at your front teeth and therefore there is less likelihood that your front teeth may be broken.*

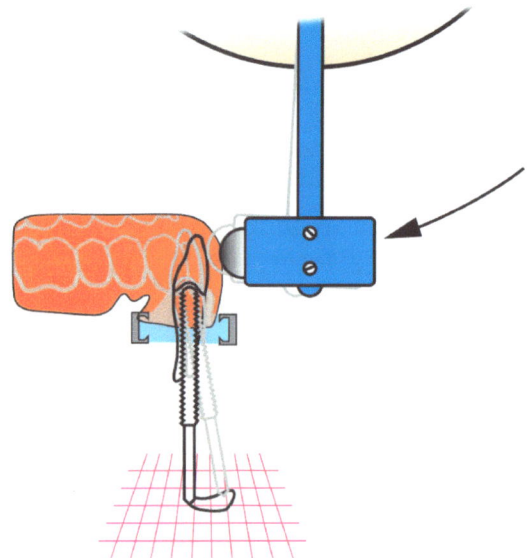

Reproduced with permission of Erkodent GmbH

Different levels of impact require mouthguards with different amounts of protection

We will talk about younger players later but, in most cases, once a person has a majority of their permanent teeth, a mouthguard should be worn that is suitable for the sport and level of competition.

Light Impact

Light Impact mouthguards are designed for lower impact sports, junior players or where helmets are worn.

Light Mouthguards may have up to 200% more cushioning and 300% more resistance to distortion than most 'Boil & Bite' mouthguards.

Medium Impact

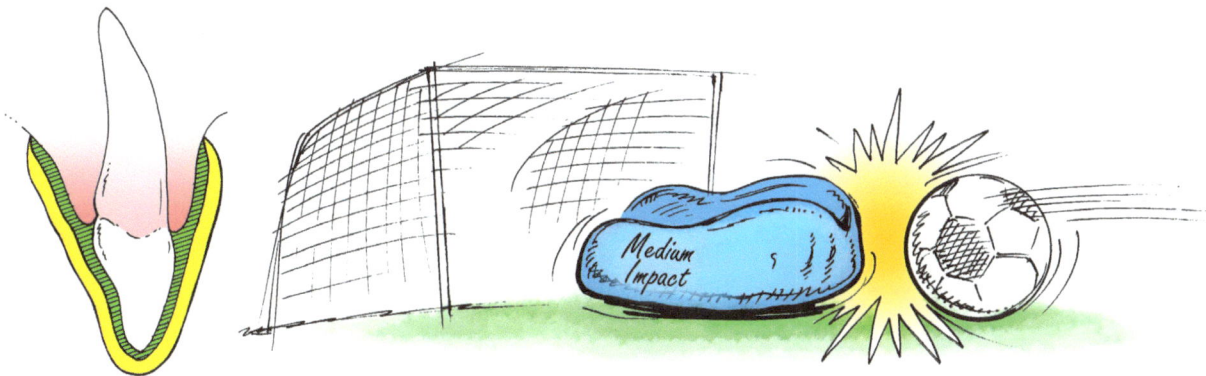

Medium mouthguards are the universal mouthguard. They are usually suitable for the majority of school and club sports where greater levels of impact are expected.

Correctly built, these mouthguards are surprisingly tough.

Medium Mouthguards may have 250% more cushioning and nearly four times more resistance to distortion than most 'Boil & Bite' mouthguards.

Heavy Impact

Impact Dispersion Bands

Sports such as Boxing, Squash and Cricket are usually suited to this level of protection. 'Heavy' impact mouthguards are often used at representative level.

Heavy Impact Mouthguards may have up to three times more cushioning and more than five times additional resistance to distortion than most 'Boil & Bite' mouthguards.

Super Heavy Impact

These are used in competition where extremely heavy impact can be expected, at representative level, for 'collision' sports or for sports using racquets or sticks.

Hard Bonded Layer

Super Heavy Mouthguards may have up to 350% more cushioning and nearly 10 times more resistance to distortion than most 'Boil & Bite' mouthguards.

Note: *Further University tests have confirmed that the Super Heavy Impact Mouthguard is **the world's most protective mouthguard design!***

If you gag or a mouthguard is too bulky or intrusive, what options do you have?

One of the great advantages of a Custom Laminated Mouthguard is that it can be modified to suit you. A new mouthguard design has been tested at the University of Tubingen. It is the same basic construction as a Super Heavy Impact Design but is produced from a thinner material.

The Tests showed that this Light Super Heavy Contact design had **31% less bulk** than a Super Heavy Impact mouthguard but may have **84% or more of the protection** (defined as: power distribution to the first molar).

Remember mouthguards designs may not be as protective when they are trimmed or modified. Wherever possible the effectiveness of a mouthguard design should be independently tested and that any deviation from that design should be undertaken with great care.

Impact pendulum test, University Tübingen: Percentage of the power reception of the first molar (power distribution).

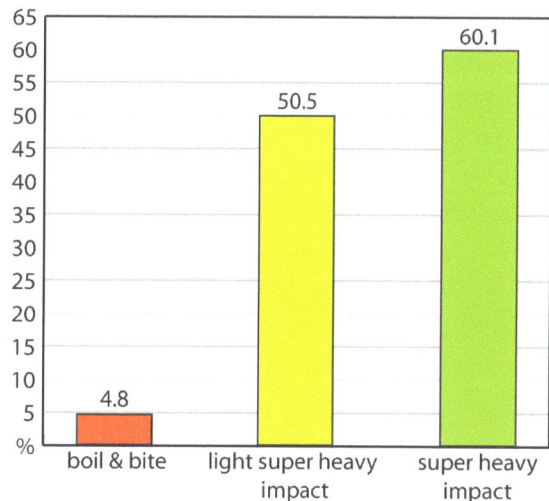

Light Super Heavy Impact

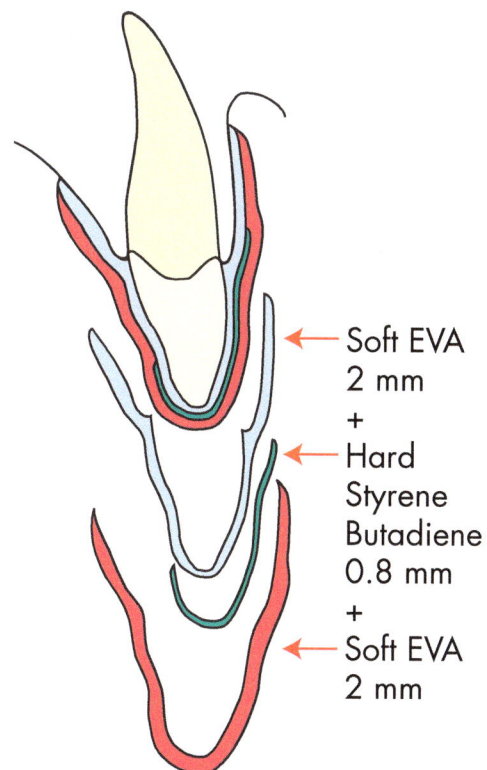

← Soft EVA 2 mm
+
← Hard Styrene Butadiene 0.8 mm
+
← Soft EVA 2 mm

Reproduced with permission of Erkodent GmbH

What protection do younger players need?

Just like adults, younger players need varying levels of protection. But younger players are the greatest challenge. Parental finances are invariably under siege, their children's dentition is rapidly changing, like the rest of their bodies and they keep on losing their mouthguards anyway.

If I were forced to wear a loose, uncomfortable mouthguard that most children have to wear, **I would try to lose it as soon as possible.** Basically… **Don't blame the children, blame the mouthguard!!**

Everyone has grown up with cheap 'Boil & Bite' mouthguards and many people have grown up with cheap, misfitting gym shoes. We do not wear cheap, misfitting gym shoes any more but *we continue to impose cheap, misfitting 'Boil & Bite' mouthguards, into the particularly sensitive mouths of children.* Having overcome the trauma and possibly, blistering in the mouth from the fitting, kids have difficulty breathing and speaking, so they get rid of the awful device as soon as they can. You cannot blame them. Blame the mouthguard.

Basically the problem is – what is perceived as important. Some consider a good mouthguard to be an unnecessary expense, while at the same time, others consider it a *vital piece of protective sporting equipment.*

<u>Parents, trainers and teachers</u> – Consider the longer term. Realise that a lot of teeth are lost in the teens. Remember, many specialists know ...

There is no doubt that if children wear mouthguards when they are young, they will continue to do so for the rest of their lives.

The formula is simple. *If mouthguards are comfortable.* They are in fun or in team colours and may have graphics, *kids will willingly wear them.* Seal their name and telephone number in the mouthguard and if it is lost, there is a good chance it will be returned.

Additional protection for younger players

Parents and sports administrators are keenly aware that younger players who compete at a ferocious pace and may not have developed the protective skills that come with age or those that play hockey and other racquet or stick sports are in greater danger.

They probably have some secondary (permanent) teeth; usually the centrals (front) that stand out and seem especially vulnerable.

The answer could be to give them the additional protection of a *Light Super Heavy Impact* design which may be more easily accepted into their smaller mouths, has a critical hard bonded layer and yet is flexible and therefore surprisingly comfortable to wear.

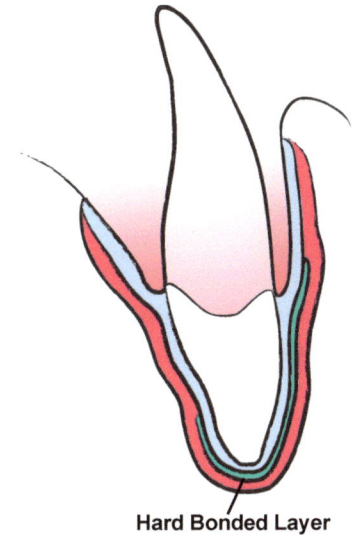

Hard Bonded Layer

Mouthguards for orthodontics

One piece of advice used to be, "If you are wearing orthodontic bands, you should not play sport". Today that's a virtual impossibility for most young people!!

Another piece of advice was, and sometimes still is, "As your teeth are changing, you should only have a cheap mouthguard".

It has also been suggested after orthodontic treatment has been completed, a mouthguard should not be worn because it may change the position of the teeth.

The reasoning is flawed. Orthodontic bands can make a mess of soft tissue! The cost of good mouthguards should be part of the treatment plan. And it is vital to provide protection.

But there is some good news. NOW you can get <u>extra protection</u> at NO EXTRA COST. With a new, stronger mouthguard material. University tests have proved that it can provide…

66% More Protection Even Over Orthodontic Bands

Dr Keith Hunter, an acknowledged expert, describes a new, more resilient material as *"The biggest single factor in producing better mouthguards for many years"*. For the technically inclined, the better mouthguard materials have a Shore A Hardness of 82. The new material has a Shore A Hardness of 95.

Tests conducted at Germany's oldest university proved that over orthodontic bands, this new thermoplastic will provide up to 66% more protection. That is a spectacular result!

The thermoforming effect (thinning on the incisal) that I described earlier, is overcome with the inclusion of an Impact Dispersion Band.

Where Super Heavy Impact Protection is required your dental or medical specialist may advise a mouthguard with lingual reinforcing that is where the hard bonded layer is placed behind your teeth.

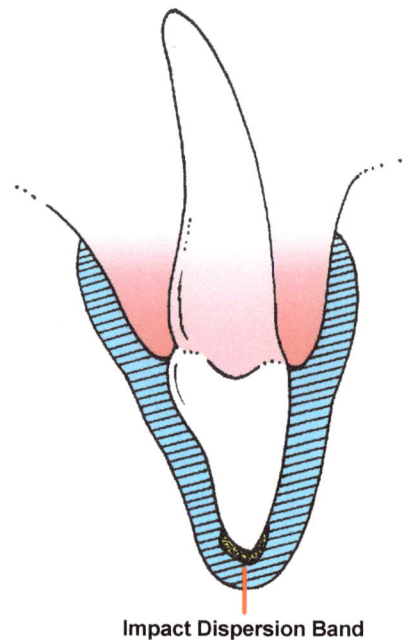

Impact Dispersion Band

You may have a false sense of protection with over the counter 'boil and bite' mouthguards

You already know that an Over the Counter 'Boil and Bite' mouthguard may have less protection and less comfort, and you may find it more difficult to breathe than with a properly made, fitted and worn custom laminated mouthguard.

A 'Boil and Bite' mouthguard, is formed by first softening it in very hot water and then placing it in the mouth and by biting, sucking and pushing the material into place.

It is at this point that you may think you have adequate protection but you would be wrong because at an international symposium as far back as 1993, Dr J Park and his fellow researchers showed that:

Boil and Bite mouthguards provide a false sense of protection due to the dramatic decrease in thickness when the athlete bites it into place during its softened state.

If air cushioning is good for car makers, is it good for mouthguards?

As carmakers use air cushions for our protection, it seems logical to do the same with mouthguards. But is it?

I experimented with air cushions in 1986 and evaluated the results at the Australian Institute of Sport. Unfortunately air cushioning in mouthguards did not work then and it does not necessarily work now. Why is this? Claims are made and some tests have shown that air cushioned materials may absorb more impact, but:

- Consider the **total cushioning** provided by the mouthguard and the shock absorbancy of the mouthguard material. University tests have indicated that most of the impact from a heavy blow **may not be absorbed** by air cushioned mouthguard material once it has been formed into a mouthguard.

- Tests also proved that the **cushioning effect rapidly decreases as impact increases** to the extent that at higher levels of impact, air cushioned mouthguards may not be much better than low level 'Boil & Bite' guards.
  However, all Custom Laminated designs, that were also tested, were **more protective** than the air cushioned mouthguards.

- In my experience it is not possible to consistently have either **accurate or adequate adaptation** to your teeth. The high heat and high forming forces, that give *vital retention* with Custom Laminated Mouthguards, have not been successfully applied to the air cushioned materials.

- Air takes more space and in the confines of the mouth. Mouthguard **bulk should be reduced** and not increased, especially with young players so they can breathe and speak easily.

Why you should take care when wearing a mouthguard with a gel liner

There are 'Boil and Bite' mouthguards that use a gel liner in an attempt to achieve a better fit. A better fit may be achieved but, would I recommend this type of mouthguard? The answer is, **take care**. Why? Compared to a properly fitted custom made mouthguard:

- Mouthguard bulk in the mouth may be increased and that is not good for breathing, speaking and other vital requirements.

In practice there may be little, and sometimes, almost an absence of bond between the mouthguard shell and the gel. Careful and skilled trimming may be necessary. Not only are protection and ability to breathe and speak reduced but there *could be a danger of ingesting part of the mouthguard*.

- There may be hygiene problems.

- Irrespective of claims that may be made, to date I know of no independent or universally accepted test results for these mouthguards.

- If you have any doubts about this type of mouthguard, show one to a dentist and ask his or her opinion.

Mouthguards for boxers

Boxers' mouthguards need to cover more teeth to take the loads caused by being frequently hit under and around the jaw.

With this modification in mind, boxers require 'Heavy' impact mouthguards whilst kick boxers need 'Super Heavy' designs.

Some boxers are being advised to wear bi-maxillary mouthguards that cover both dental arches. These are welded together while leaving a hole for breathing. Amongst dental specialists there are differing opinions about the safety and protectiveness of this type of guard.

What additional features are required for boxers?

- Boxers need a mouthguard with a slightly thicker outside (labial) surface.

- The mouthguard should be extended to cover the 2nd molars.

- According to Dr Keith Hunter there should be 4 mm of material covering the occlusal surface (the biting surface).

- The mouthguard should be adjusted by imprinting the lower teeth in the mouthguard (forming an occlusal table) to absorb and spread more impact.

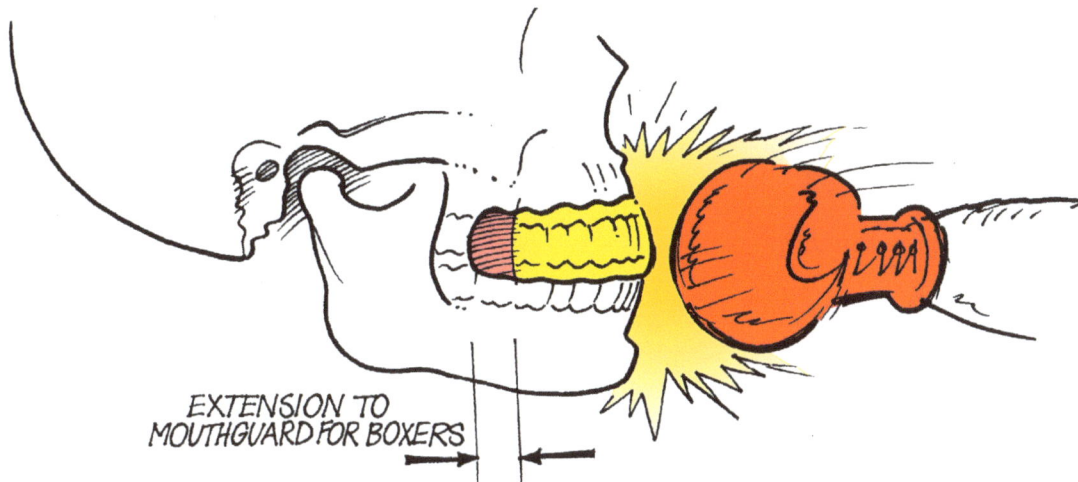

EXTENSION TO
MOUTHGUARD FOR BOXERS

What additional features are required for water polo players?

The answer is simple. Wear a mouthguard that:

- Won't get knocked out. Custom laminated mouthguards are proven to have the best retention.

- Floats. Again custom laminated are the best.

- Is correctly balanced so that you do not ingest water and you can breathe easily.

- Is made in a high visibility colour.

Which mouthguard should you wear?

Did you know that some well known Formula 1 Racing Drivers wear mouthguards when they are racing? They wear a 'Light' impact design that protects their teeth, increases upper body strength and reduces fatigue. They need protection but, because they wear helmets they do not need a 'Heavy' impact mouthguard.

In comparison international Rugby Union players, Hockey players and Kick Boxers with little head and face protection, need 'Super Heavy' protection. The highest they can get!

The level of protection you need may change. Therefore the protection you get from the mouthguard you wear needs to change depending on

- The sport you play

- Your age and weight

- The level of competition

- Other factors such as

    - Orthodontic bands

    - Missing teeth

    - Occlusal irregularities

    - Personal features including medical or dental factors

The selection of any mouthguard is ultimately your decision and your choice. So, in addition to essential **professional dental and medical advice** read:

- "25 Reasons Why You Can Get More Protection, More Comfort and More Choice With A Custom Laminated Mouthguard Than With Any Other Mouthguard"

- "Guide To The Minimum Levels Of Protection For 46 Sports"

How often should a mouthguard be changed?

I am often asked this question. It may depend on how well you care for your mouthguard. These are some general guidelines:

- For children – *Annually or whenever their dentition changes to the extent that the mouthguard does not fit.*
  Note: *Most good custom laminated mouthguards are adjustable! Although, unfortunately, not those with a hard bonded layer.*

- For club players – *Preferably every year but if not every 2 years providing the mouthguard still fits and is appropriate to the level of risk.*
  Much depends on the materials that are used.

- For professional and heavy impact sports – *Annually and, after an exceptionally heavy impact, get a new mouthguard.*
  Cars are taken to crash repairers after an accident. Mouthguards, after exceptional impact, are little different.

What other factors should be considered?

We have now looked at many of the factors affecting dental injuries in sport as well as the benefits for you with a good custom laminated mouthguard.

There are risk factors that are specifically related to particular sports. Amongst these consider:

- Rules of the sport

- Coaching methods

- The attitude of other players

- Equipment

- Personal equipment

- Refereeing

- First aid facilities (Learn the steps to save a tooth if it is knocked out)

Wear your mouthguard at training because many injuries are caused when training

You spend more time training than competing. So it is logical to wear a mouthguard when training.

How many people have missed selection or performed below standard after a training injury? Don't join them. The recommendation by specialists is unanimous, **Wear Your Mouthguard at Training!**

What should you expect to receive with your mouthguard?

With a custom laminated mouthguard, your name and telephone number should be permanently sealed inside. It should be supplied with a strong, <u>ventilated</u> container. It should have printed care instructions.

Caring for your mouthguard

These are the generally accepted guidelines to care for your mouthguard:

- Rinse well before use

- Wash in cold soapy water after each use and rinse under cold water

- Store in a ventilated container

- Do not place in direct sunlight or in hot water

- Do not let others use your mouthguard

- If it feels dry in your mouth, apply a thin film of petroleum jelly

- If it becomes loose, tight or causes any discomfort contact the specialist or organisation that supplied it.

Summary – this is what you now know

- You now know how a mouthguard is designed with a view to reducing dental injury. How it can be more comfortable, and how it can help to improve your performance.

- We have looked at different types of mouthguards and the protection these may give you.

- You know some of the reasons why it is my opinion that the best protection you can have is with a custom laminated mouthguard that has been formed under pressure or with a high vacuum reservoir machine.

- You know a good mouthguard can do more than just stop a tooth being chipped. You know that **fit and retention are vital factors** for your safety.

- Now you know you should have the protection of a properly made custom laminated mouthguard that is effectively, two or three mouthguards in one.

- You understand the major reasons some mouthguards may provide more protection and you know you can be discerning about what you are being sold!!

- No longer do you have to be one of the 82% who wear a mouthguard that is an accident waiting to happen!

Now, when you wear a better mouthguard, you will find that:

The more comfortable you are, the better you can breathe and speak, and the greater protection you have, the better you are going to play!!!

Enjoy your game.

Julian Hodges
Avalon, Australia

25 Reasons Why there is More Protection, More Comfort and You Play Better with a Custom Laminated Mouthguard

A Direct Comparison With Some Over the Counter 'Boil and Bite' Mouthguards

Custom Laminated Mouthguard	Over the Counter 'Boil and Bite' Mouthguard
Design	**Design**
Your mouthguard will be designed and custom made *for you* 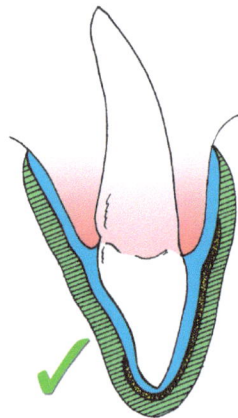	**Design *cannot* change** 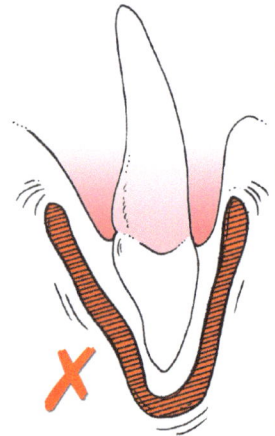
✓ Design can be changed depending upon:	✗ Design is inflexible
• Your age and physical stature	✗ You may be forced to wear an inappropriate mouthguard
• The sport you play	✗ Modification either severely limited or not possible
• The level of competition	
✓ Allows modification for your special needs, such as:	
• Orthodontic bands	
• Irregularities to your teeth or bite	
• Missing teeth	

Custom Laminated Mouthguards	Over the Counter 'Boil and Bite' Mouthguards
Manufacture	**Manufacture**
✓ Custom made in a specialised laboratory under high heat and pressure	✗ Injection moulded in a factory
Fit	**Fit**
Precise fit is vital for your mouthguard.	*It is Difficult if not Impossible to Get Good Fit with an 'Over the Counter' Mouthguard.*
A good custom laminated mouthguard will give you micron accurate fit that should:	*Poor fit may give you these problems:*
✓ Provide a better cushioning effect	✗ Reduced protection
✓ Make it easier to breathe	✗ Breathing difficulties
✓ Make it easier to talk	✗ Speech difficulties
✓ Provide more comfort and be easier to wear	✗ Less comfort
✓ Make it more difficult to dislodge on impact	✗ It may be easily dislodged
✓ Allow you to concentrate and give you confidence when you wear it.	✗ You can ingest it
	✗ You can be distracted
	✗ Even your dentist cannot improve the retention in your mouth
Occlusal Table	**Occlusal Table**
For adults the imprint of your lower jaw in your mouthguard is important because:	*No occlusal table and therefore:*
✓ Risk of being concussed can be reduced	✗ There is a greater risk of injury
✓ Risk of damage to your jaw joint (TMJ) can be reduced	
✓ Risk of fracturing your jaw can be reduced	
✓ There is a better spread of impact	
✓ It helps protect your bottom teeth.	

Custom Laminated Mouthguards	Over the Counter 'Boil and Bite' Mouthguards
Testing ✓ Independent University tests have proved that, correctly constructed, this type of mouthguard may provide more protection than any other.	**Testing** ✗ Test protocols have not objectively measured the total function of a 'Boil and Bite' mouthguard.
Construction ✓ Laminating results in a totally bonded mouthguard that gives more protection but without discomfort	**Construction** ✗ Some 'Boil and Bite' mouthguards have hard inserts that can break off ✗ Many 'Boil and Bite' mouthguards are too soft or too thin
Approval ✓ Recommended by national dental associations worldwide. ✓ Universal approval by dentists and University research staff	**Approval** ✗ Not recommended/preferred by national dental associations ✗ No universal approval
Colours & Special Effects *You can have* ✓ Wide choice of colours ✓ Multi-colours or your Team's Colours ✓ Your sponsors' logos ✓ Special effects	**Colours & Special Effects** ✗ Limited choice of colours ✗ Multi and Team colours not available ✗ Sponsor's logos and special effects are rarely available, if at all.
Additional Features *You mouthguard can feature:* ✓ Your name ✓ Your telephone number ✓ A protective description of your mouthguard	**Additional Features** ✗ None

Conclusion:

4 Vital Benefits of a Custom Laminated Mouthguard

- More Protection
- More Comfort
- More Choice
- You Play Better

Note: *There may be differences for young players*

Guide to the Minimum Levels of Protection for 46 Sports

It is essential that you read the Notes to this Guide.

Sport	Degree of Impact or Collision			
	Light	Medium	Heavy or Light Super Heavy	Super Heavy
Mouthguard Construction				
Acrobatics		✓		
American Football		✓		
Australian Rules Football		✓		
Baseball		✓		
Basketball		✓		
BMX (wearing a helmet)	✓			
Boxing (See Notes)			✓	
Cricket			✓	
Equestrian		✓		
Field Hockey				✓
Gaelic Football		✓		
Gymnastics		✓		
Handball		✓		
Horse Riding		✓		
Hurling				✓
Ice Hockey				✓
Indoor Cricket		✓		
In-Line Skating		✓		
Kick Boxing (See Notes)				✓
Lacrosse				✓
Martial Arts (See Notes)		✓		

Sport	Degree of Impact or Collision			
	Light	Medium	Heavy or Light Super Heavy	Super Heavy
Motor Cross (wearing a helmet)	✓			
Motor Racing (wearing a helmet)	✓			
Netball		✓		
Polo and Polocrosse				✓
Racquetball				✓
Roller Hockey				✓
Rollerblading			✓	
Rounders		✓		
Rugby League		✓		
Rugby Union		✓		
Shot Putting		✓		
Skateboarding			✓	
Skiing		✓		
Ski Racing			✓	
Skydiving		✓		
Soccer		✓		
Softball		✓		
Squash			✓	
Surfing		✓		
T Ball		✓		
Touch Football		✓		
Volleyball		✓		
Water Polo		✓		
Weightlifting		✓		
Wrestling		✓		

Notes:

This is a Guide ONLY. Players may require greater levels of protection and it may not be possible to eliminate all injury. The protective level required will change dependant upon a number of factors including, but not limited to, the level and intensity of competition and the competitive nature of the sports person. **Specialist dental and medical advice is recommended.**

Boxing, kick boxing, some martials arts and other Heavy and Super Heavy 'Collision' sports or contact may require mouthguards with greater coverage of the occlusal surfaces of the teeth.

In some sports, it may be appropriate for younger players with deciduous teeth to have lighter impact mouthguards.

This Guide should be read in conjunction with *"82% Of Mouthguards Are An Accident Waiting To Happen"(page 8), and "25 Reasons Why There is More Protection, More Comfort and You Play Better With A Custom Laminated Mouthguard" (page 30)* **and with dental and medical advice.**

References

1. American Dental Association Council on Dental Materials – Association Reports. Mouth protectors and sports team dentists. J Am Dent Assoc 1984; 109: 84-7.

2. Aubry M, Cantu R, Dvorak J, Graf-Baumann T, Johnston K, Kelly J, M Lovell, McCrory P, Meeuwisse W, and Schamasch P. Summary and agreement statement of the first International Conference on Concussion in Sport, Vienna 2001. Br. J. Sports Med., Feb 2002; 36: 6 – 7

3. Banky J & McCrory P. Mouthguard Use in Australian Sport. J Sci Med Sport 1999; 2(1): 20-29

4. 'Brisbane Schoolboy Swallows Mouthguard' Sunday Mail, Brisbane Australia. 25 June 1995.

5. Chapman PJ. Concussion in contact sports and importance of mouthguards in protection. Aust J Sci Med Sport March 1985: 23-7.

6. Chapman PJ. The Prevalence of orofacial injuries and use of mouthguards in rugby union. Aust Dent J 1985; 30:364-7.

7. Cotton FR, Mouth protection: the healthy choice – Can Dent Hyg 1985; 19(1): 16-9.

8. Croll TP, Castaldi CR. The custom fitted athletic mouthguard for the orthodontic patient and for the child with mixed dentition. Quintess Int 1989; 20(8): 571-5.

9. Davis GT, Knott SC. Dental trauma in Australia. Aust Dent J 1984; 29(4): 217-21.

10. De Wet FA. The prevention of orofacial injuries in the adolescent. Int Dent J 1981; 31(4): 313-9.

11. Dental Injury Fact Sheet. National Youth Sports Foundation for the Prevention of Athletic Injury Inc. Needham, Mass, 1992.

12. Deyoung AK, Robinson E, Goodwin WC. Comparing comfort and wearability: custom-made vs self-adapted mouthguards. J Am Dent Assoc 1994; 125(8): 1112-8.

13. Finch C, Braham R, McIntosh A, McCrory P, Wolfe R. Should football players wear custom-fitted mouthguards? – Results from a group randomized controlled trial. *Injury Prevention* 2005; 11: 242 – 246

14. Flanders, Raymond A., Mohondas Bhat. The incidence of orofacial injuries in sports, a pilot study in Illinios. J. Am Dent Assoc 1985; 126: 491-6.

15. Football injuries to the head and neck, National Health and Medical Research Council of Australia. 1995. 59-60; 108-111.

16. Harcourt JK. Sporting injuries – are they preventable? Aust Dent J 1989; 485-6.

17. Healey D. Legal liability in sport. 'Play It Safe' Conference . NSW Dept Sport Rec, Sydney, Australia, Nov 1998.

18. Henne P. Tests to determine the effect of various polishing agents on mouthguard material. Unpublished data 1994. ACL" GmbH, Rottenberg, Germany.

19. Heuchart W, Kirschmann W, Hodges J, Kopp HP. Test Procedure: DIN/150 53512, 51225. International test arrangement for measuring return energy of elastomers or foams. Pfalzgrafenweiler, Germany. Unpublished data: August 1994.

20. Hodges J, Burns P. Making a pressure formed mouthguard. Dental Outlook. Dent Health Foundation – Australia 1985: 11(1): 15-7.

21. Hodges J. New custom laminated mouthguards can provide high levels of protection and comfort. Australian Sports Trainer: March 1996: 4-7.

22. Hoffman J, Alfter G, Rudolph NK, Göz G. Experimental comparative study of various types of mouthguards. Endod Dent Traumatol 1999: 15: 157-163.

23. Hunter K. Modern mouthguards. Dental Outlook, Dental Health Foundation – Australia 1989; 15(3): 63-67.

24. Hunter K. Sports Mouthguards. Dental Health Foundation – Australia 1997.

25. Johnson DC, Winters JE. Prevention of intraoral trauma in sports. Dent Clin North Am 1991; 35(4) 657-66.

26. Kennedy D. Childrens sport, risks and liabilities. 'Play It Safe' Conference. NSW Dept Sport Rec, Sydney, Australia, Nov 1998.

27. Maeda Y, Emura I, Onoue Y, Maeda N, Okada M, Nokubi Tet a, Okino Y. Mouthguards and occlusal force distribution. J Osaka Dent Sch 1990; 30: 125-30.

28. Maestrello C L, Mourino A P, Farrington F H, Dentists' attitudes towards mouthguard protection. Pediatr Dent. 1999 Sep-Oct; 21(6): 340-6.

29. Maile S. Comparison between boil and bite and custom laminated mouthguards. University of Tubingen. Unpublished data 1996.

30. McCrory P, Johnston K, Meeuwisse W, Aubry M, Cantu R, Dvorak J, Graf-Baumann T, Kelly J, Lovell M, and Schamasch P. Summary and agreement statement of the 2nd International Conference on Concussion in Sport, Prague 2004. Br. J. Sports Med., Apr 2005; 39: 196 – 204

31. McNamara C, 'Mouthguards dangerous" Sunday Mail, Brisbane Australia. 2 July 1995.

32. Nysether S. Dental injuries among Norwegian soccer players. Comm Dent Oral Epidemiol 1987; 15: 141-3.

33. Padilla R, S. Sports Dentistry and prevention of oral injuries, CDA Sessions, Annaheim, California, May 12 1995.

34. Padilla R, Balikov S. Sports dentistry coming of age in the 90's. J Calif Dent Assoc April 1993: 27-34.

35. Park et al, Methods of improved mouthguards, First International Symposium on Biomaterials, Taejon, Korea, August 1993.

36. Park J, Scholl KL, Overton B, Darley KJ, Improving mouthguards. J Prosth Dent 1994; 72: 373-80.

37. Rasalli DN. Prevention of craniofacial injuries in football. Dent Clin. North Am 1991; 35(4): 627-45.

38. Rocky Mountain Regional Brain Injury Centre. A manual for the assessment and management of concussion/brain injury in sports.

39. Rudoff N. The travelling of impact power through the upper dental arch comparing different mouthguard constructions. University of Tubingen. Unpublished data 1997.

40. Schwanzer DA. Comparison of different mouthguards over orthodontic appliances. University of Tubingen. Unpublished data 1997.

41. Soporowski NJ, Tesini DA, Weiss AJ. Survey of orofacial sports-related injuries. J Mass Dent Soc 1994; 43 (4): 16-20.

42. Spillane DM. Dentists, mouthguards, and the law. J Mass Dent Soc 1994; 43 (4): 21-4.

43. Sports injuries in Australia – Causes, costs and prevention. Australian Better Health Program 1990.

44. Standards Australia International Limited, Guidelines for the fabrication, use and maintenance of sports mouthguards. HB 209 - 2003

45. Stenger JM. Mouthguards: prevention against shock to head, neck and teeth. J Am Dent Assoc 1964; 69:273-281.

46. Stokes ANF, Croft GC, Gee D. Comparison of laboratory and intraorally formed mouth protectors. Endod Dent Traumatol 1987; 3: 255-8.

www.ingramcontent.com/pod-product-compliance
Lightning Source LLC
Chambersburg PA
CBHW061058090426

42742CB00002B/83